3 1994 01259 3494

SANTA SANTA ANA RARY
PUBLIC LIBRARY
NEW HOPE

D0537321

RELIGIONS OF
THE MIDDLE EAST

By Cory Gunderson

J 200.956 GUN
Gunderson, Cory Gideon
Religions of the Middle
   East
      JAN 2 5 2005
                        $25.65
BOOKMOBILE 1   31994012593494

VISIT US AT
WWW.ABDOPUB.COM

Published by ABDO & Daughters, an imprint of ABDO Publishing
Company, 4940 Viking Drive, Suite 622, Edina, Minnesota 55435.
Copyright ©2004 by Abdo Consulting Group, Inc. International
copyrights reserved in all countries. No part of this book may be
reproduced in any form without written permission from the publisher.

Printed in the United States.

Edited by: Sheila Rivera
Contributing Editors: Paul Joseph, Chris Schafer
Graphic Design: Arturo Leyva, David Bullen
Cover Design: Castaneda Dunham, Inc.
Photos: Corbis, Fotosearch

Library of Congress Cataloging-in-Publication Data

Gunderson, Cory Gideon.
    Religions of the Middle East / Cory Gunderson.
      p. cm. -- (World in conflict--the Middle East)
    Includes index.
    Contents: Overview of Middle Eastern Religions -- Islam -- Christianity -- Judaism --
    Hinduism -- Druze.
      ISBN 1-59197-412-7
        1. Middle East--Religion--Juvenile literature. [1. Middle East--Religion. 2. Religions.] I
    Title. II. World in conflict (Edina, Minn.). Middle East.

    BL1060.G86 2003
    200'.956--dc21

                                                                            200304184€

TABLE OF CONTENTS

Israeli settlers

OVERVIEW OF MIDDLE EASTERN RELIGIONS

Islam, Christianity, and Judaism are major world religions. They are the three major religions of the Middle East, too. All were born in the Middle East. All three are monotheistic. This means that each religion believes in just one God. These religions have much in common. Christianity was launched from within the Jewish religion. Islam developed from both Judaism and Christianity. All three view Abraham as their religion's first prophet. For this reason, Islam, Christianity, and Judaism are also called the Abrahamic religions.

Though these three religions share much in common, their differences have resulted in great suffering. This has been especially true in the Middle East. Much of the Middle East conflict is rooted in one religion's intolerance of another.

This intolerance has played out in the Israeli-Palestinian conflict. World War II left many Jews isolated and homeless.

Symbols representing major Middle East religions

Jews were released from concentration camps across Europe with no nation to call their own. Many of them moved to the Middle Eastern land called Palestine. Britain had control over Palestine at that time. British leaders knew that the Islamic Arabs and the Jews both wanted the land. The United Nations decided to divide the land. This organization's role is to promote peace throughout the world. The UN decided to create separate Jewish and Islamic states.

The Arab people were very angry about the UN decision. They wanted all of Palestine and the Middle East land for their fellow Arab Muslims. On May 15, 1948, Egypt, Syria, Iraq, Lebanon, Jordan, and Saudi Arabia declared war on Israel. Israel successfully defended itself. Still, the Arab nations refused to recognize Israel as an independent Jewish nation. The Jewish people did not wait for Arab acceptance. They moved into the region now known as Israel and forced many Palestinians from their homes.

Israeli Jews continue to live in and control land that once belonged to Palestine. Angry Palestinian Islamic extremists respond by bombing Jewish targets. The Israeli people continue to fight back. A solution to this conflict seems unlikely in the near future.

It is helpful to note how small the Jewish population is in the Middle East. It is especially small compared to the Muslim population. Currently almost 5,000,000 Jews live in the Middle East. About 217,000,000 Muslims live in countries of the Middle

RELIGIONS OF THE MIDDLE EAST

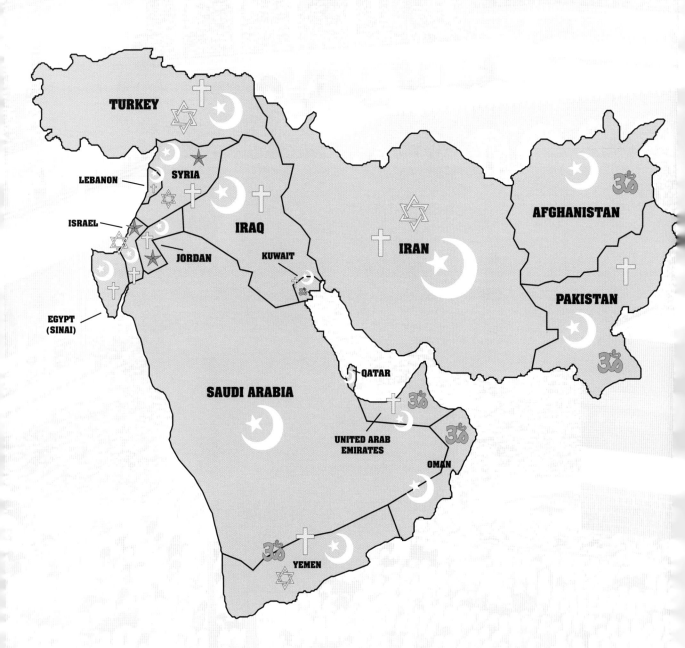

Of all the people living in the Middle East:

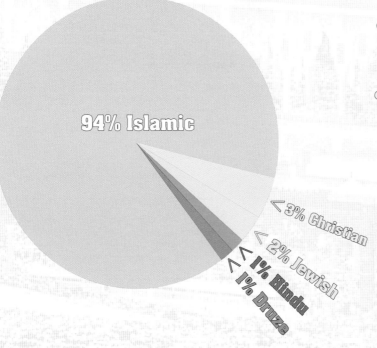

94% Islamic

‹ 3% Christian

‹ 2% Jewish

‹ 1% Hindu
‹ 1% Druze

- **94% are Islamic**

- Less than
3% are Christian

- Less than
2% are Jewish

- Less than
1% are Druze

- Less than
1% are Hindu

The Earth has more than 6 billion people:

- About 33% are Christians

- About 25% are Islamic

- About 15% are Hindu

- About 14% are non-religious

- About 6% are Buddhist

- The other 7% have different beliefs

 ISLAM ✝ CHRISTIANITY

 DRUZE HINDUISM JUDAISM

East. There are also about 5,500,000 Christians that live in the Middle East. Hinduism and Druze are two other religions practiced in the Middle East, but only in small numbers. There are about 740,000 Middle Eastern Hindus and 595,000 Druze. The following chapters explore these religions.

Israeli soldiers and Palestinian civilians

ISLAM

The Prophet Muhammad began the Islamic religion. He was born in 570 A.D. in Mecca, Saudi Arabia. When Muhammad was 40, he began to hear messages from Allah. Allah is the Arabic word for God. Muslims believe that Muhammad was the final prophet of Allah. A prophet is someone who God speaks through directly. Muslims believe Muhammad was a human being, rather than a holy spirit or the son of Allah.

Muhammad was disgusted by the citizens of Mecca he saw drinking and gambling. He didn't like seeing the women and children of Mecca being treated badly. He left Mecca around 610. In 622, Muhammad and his followers settled in the city of Medina, Saudi Arabia. Muslims were offered religious freedom there. The move to Medina was so important that the Islamic calendar was set according to it. This calendar follows the cycles of the moon.

Some people wrote down the messages sent from Allah that were spoken by Muhammad. The collection of these messages makes up the Islamic holy book called the Koran.

Muslims live their lives according to the Five Pillars of Islam. These pillars are the foundation of the Islamic religion. The five pillars are: faith, prayer, charity, fasting, and pilgrimage.

The first pillar, called Shahada, tells Muslims to have faith in Allah and his teachings. The second pillar is called the Salat. Salat are the prayers that Muslims must say at dawn, noon, mid-afternoon, sunset, and nightfall. Muslims can pray at home, at work, or in a mosque. The mosque is the Muslim place of worship. The third pillar is called the Zakat. Zakat requires Muslims to give at least 2.2 percent of their own wealth to charity each year. The fourth pillar is the Sawm, or the fast. Every year, during the month of Ramadan, Muslims go without food or water during daylight hours. They do this to cleanse themselves. The fifth pillar is the pilgrimage, or Hajj. Each Muslim who is able should travel to Mecca at least once in his or her lifetime. They travel during the holy month of Ramadan to pray with other Muslims.

Because the Islamic year is based on lunar cycles, Ramadan falls sometimes in the summer and sometimes in the winter. Muslims celebrate the end of Hajj with a festival called Eid al-Adha. Muslims everywhere pray and exchange gifts as part of this celebration.

Mecca was a holy city even before the creation of Islam. People went to Mecca to worship at a large, cube-shaped temple called the Ka'ba. Mecca later became the Muslims' holy place because that is where the prophet Muhammad was born.

Portrait of the Prophet Muhammad

After Muhammad's death, Muslims were divided in deciding who should be their next leader. This decision split Muslims into two major groups, the Sunnis and the Shiites.

The Sunnis make up the largest group of Muslims. The first Sunnis believed that tribal elders should choose the person to lead after Muhammad. They wanted to choose the most powerful person within their religion. Following this tradition today, any Sunni Muslim can lead as long as he is qualified. He must also be a good Muslim. Sunni Muslims do not think that their leaders require or possess sacred wisdom.

Shiites are in the minority as they make up only 10 percent of the Muslim population. The first Shiites believed that Muhammad's successor should come from within the Prophet's family. These Muslims chose Ali, Muhammad's cousin and son-in-law, to lead them. Today, Shiite Muslims continue to believe that only relatives of the Prophet Muhammad are qualified to be Muslim leaders, or caliphs. Shiites feel that the title of caliph should be handed down from one male family member to the next. Shiites believe caliphs have sacred wisdom because they descended from the holy family.

The Islamic religion has suffered in recent years because of the actions of radical Islamic fundamentalists. Radical fundamentalists can also be called extremists. They believe the Koran allows them to violently attack non-Muslims in order to defend Islam. The majority of Muslims do not believe that the Koran permits violence.

Worldwide, an estimated 1.2 to 1.3 billion people are Muslim. That makes Islam the second most practiced religion in the world. Muslims make up one fifth of the world's population.

Muslim pilgrims face the Ka'ba inside the Grand Mosque during sunset prayers.

CHRISTIANITY

The Christian religion began with the birth of a man called Jesus. Christians believe that Jewish scripture predicted Jesus' birth many years earlier. Christians believe Jesus' mother, Mary, was a virgin when she gave birth to him. Jesus grew up in the town of Nazareth, which is in present day Israel. Jesus Christ, Lord, and Jesus of Nazareth are titles used to identify Jesus.

Jesus was so important that a new calendar was set from the year of his birth. This became known as the Gregorian calendar. The initials B.C. mean the years before Christ's birth. The initials A.D. stand for Anno Domini. This phrase means "In the year of our Lord." These initials mark the time after Jesus' birth. Jesus was born in Bethlehem around the year 0.

Jesus spent the adult years of his life working as a carpenter. During these years, the nation of Israel was under the rule of the Roman Empire. When Jesus was in his 30s, he began teaching the word of God. He also performed miracles. Jesus attracted hundreds of followers with the following key messages:

Jesus was crucified by the Romans.

- God loves you and is always with you.
- Love one another.
- Each person has immense value.
- The good news is that the kingdom of God has come to earth (in the form of Jesus and his teachings).
- Each person will be judged at the end of his life and sent to heaven or hell.
- God forgives those who ask for forgiveness.

Jewish leaders heard that Jesus was claiming to be God. They felt that his claims violated Jewish law. These leaders asked the Roman government to kill Jesus. The Romans took Jesus to court several times. They could not convict Jesus because he was not guilty of breaking Roman law. Jewish religious leaders finally convinced Roman Governor Pontius Pilate to kill Jesus. The Romans tortured Jesus and nailed him to a cross. This form of killing is called a crucifixion.

More than 500 people reported seeing Jesus alive after his death. This caused even more people to become followers of Jesus' teachings.

Followers of Jesus' teachings created the Jewish Christian movement in Jerusalem. A man named Paul led this sect of Judaism. Paul's followers grew quickly in numbers. These followers were often tortured because of their beliefs.

When Roman Emperor Constantine became a Christian in 324 A.D., this torture ended. Later that century, Christianity became the official religion of Rome. The Roman Empire became the Holy Roman Empire. Two hundred years after that, Christian churches replaced the temples of Greek gods.

Paul and other writers recorded Jesus' life in the Christian holy book called the Bible. The Bible is divided into two main sections. The first is called the Old Testament. In addition to other books, it contains the first five books of the Jewish holy book, the Torah. The second is called the New Testament. The New Testament recorded the birth and teachings of Jesus.

The cornerstone of Christian faith is the Apostles' Creed. Its name reflects Christians' belief that Jesus' 12 apostles, the first followers, authored it. It was written sometime between the second and ninth centuries. This statement of faith says:

> I believe in God, the Father almighty,
> creator of heaven and earth.
> I believe in Jesus Christ, God's only Son, our Lord,
> who was conceived by the Holy Spirit,
> born of the Virgin Mary,
> suffered under Pontius Pilate,
> was crucified, died and was buried;
> he descended to the dead.
> On the third day he rose again;
> he ascended into heaven,
> he is seated at the right hand of the Father,
> and he will come again to judge the living and the dead.

Some Christians worship in cathedrals, like the Notre Dame Cathedral shown here.

I believe in the Holy Spirit,
the holy catholic church,
the communion of saints,
the forgiveness of sins,
the resurrection of the body,
and the life everlasting. Amen.

Different denominations have different versions of the Apostles' Creed. Christians believe that Jesus is the son of God. They believe he came to earth to save all who believe in him. Christians also believe that their sins will be forgiven if they ask God for forgiveness. They have faith that they will go to heaven after they die.

Christians believe Jerusalem to be a holy city because that is where Jesus died and rose from the dead. They worship in churches or cathedrals. Cathedrals are large, important, often highly decorated churches. Christmas and Easter are the two main Christian holidays. Christmas, which falls each year on December 25, celebrates Jesus' birth. Easter celebrates the day Jesus rose into heaven after his death.

Christianity is a divided faith. To date, there are over 1,000 Christian denominations. A denomination is a large group of religious congregations that share a common faith and name. Catholic, Lutheran, Presbyterian, and Baptist are but a few Christian denominations.

Various Christian images

Christians can be grouped into broad categories ranging from conservative to liberal. These categories help describe how strictly each group follows what the Bible says. Conservative Christians follow the Bible in the strictest, most conservative, sense. Evangelical churches and Christian fundamentalists are often described as conservative. A very small fraction of fundamentalists use violence to defend their beliefs.

On the opposite end of the spectrum are liberal Christians. Liberals believe that the Bible has different meaning today than it did when it was written. They see more room than conservatives do for different opinions on the Bible's meaning. They are not as bound to Biblical traditions as the conservatives are. Any Christian church likely includes a range of believers from conservatives to liberals.

Christianity has become the most practiced religion in the world. An estimated two billion people identify themselves as Christian. This is about one third of the world's population.

JUDAISM

Judaism is one of the oldest surviving religions. It is the oldest monotheistic religion in existence. It began more than 4,000 years ago with a man named Abraham. Abraham lived in a Middle Eastern region known as Mesopotamia. This region is located in the modern day country of Iraq.

The Jews consider Abraham to be one of God's original prophets. God spoke to Abraham several times. He told Abraham to move to a land called Cannan. Cannan later became known as Israel. God told Abraham that if he and his followers agreed to worship God alone, God would make their country great.

During Abraham's life, people throughout the Middle East worshiped several different gods. Abraham tried to convince them that there was only one true God. He told his followers they should pray to only that one God. The Jews moved to Egypt. Several years later, they were forced into slavery there.

Moses, another messenger of God, set the Jewish people free. He was the adopted son of an Egyptian princess. God spoke to Moses. He told him to free his people from their slavery under

Hebrew tablets

Egyptian rule. God sent terrible plagues upon the Egyptians. Eventually, the Egyptians released the Jews.

Moses led his people to the Sinai desert where God spoke to him again. Sinai is in the northeastern part of Egypt. Moses climbed Mount Sinai and returned 40 days later. He brought two stone tablets back with him. Ten Commandments were carved into the tablets. The Israelites placed the tablets in a box called the Ark of the Covenant. They carried the box with them as they traveled. Following are the commandments:

1. I am the Lord thy God. Thou shalt not have strange Gods before me.
2. Thou shalt not take the name of the Lord thy God in vain.
3. Remember thou keep holy the Sabbath day.
4. Honor thy father and thy mother.
5. Thou shalt not kill.
6. Thou shalt not commit adultery.
7. Thou shalt not steal.
8. Thou shalt not bear false witness against thy neighbor.
9. Thou shalt not covet thy neighbor's wife.
10. Thou shalt not covet thy neighbor's goods.

The Ten Commandments are an important part of the Jewish holy book, the Torah. The Torah was written on scrolls. Inside synagogues, Jewish places of worship, the scrolls are kept in a container. This container, called an ark, looks like a display case. The ark is the central, most important, focal point in all synagogues. It is placed on the eastern wall of synagogues so that it faces the city of Jerusalem.

Models of the Ten Commandments are set on the wall above the ark. An embroidered curtain is placed in front of them. Near the ark, a light burns continuously. During a Jewish service, men from the congregation are asked to read from the Torah. People with the last name Cohen always read first. This tradition honors the priests named Cohen who worshiped in the first temple in Jerusalem.

A second Jewish religious book is the Talmud. This book contains a collection of the teachings of early Jewish sages, or men of wisdom. The Talmud also contains written discussion by Jewish teachers. The book's purpose is to teach people about Jewish laws, customs, and religious life.

Jewish people today celebrate some of the same holy days they did in Biblical times. Probably the most important of these is Yom Kippur, or "Day of Atonement." Once a year, Jews set aside a day to atone for their sins against God. They reflect on how they've sinned during the past year. As a way to apologize to God, the Jewish people fast for 25 hours. They do not eat or drink anything during this time.

The holiday Rosh Hashanah marks the beginning of the Jewish new year. It is a time of quiet reflection and joyful celebration. Rosh Hashanah falls on the first and second days of Tishri, the seventh month in the Hebrew calendar. On the Gregorian calendar, it falls sometime in the month of September.

A Jewish Menorah

Hanukkah, another Jewish holiday, celebrates the Jews' victory over the Greek army in 165 B.C. The Greek army had taken over the Jews' holy temple in Jerusalem three years earlier. The Greeks destroyed parts of the temple as well as important holy items within it. After the Jews reclaimed, cleaned, and repaired the temple, they rededicated it to God. Hanukkah is still celebrated today and is also called the Festival of Lights. It is celebrated for eight days and nights starting on the 25th of Kislev on the Hebrew calendar. Kislev falls in either November or December on the Gregorian calendar depending on the year.

Judaism is made up of three different groups of followers. The first group is called Orthodox. Most Orthodox Jews live in Israel. These Jews follow the teachings of the Torah strictly. They believe that men and women should worship separately. Women have a very limited role in Orthodox synagogues. Orthodox Jews participate in three prayer services a day. They can pray at home, in a synagogue, or in any other place they choose. At least 10 men must be present for a prayer service to be conducted in a synagogue.

The other two major groups within the Jewish faith are the conservative and reform groups. Conservative Jews honor traditional Jewish law. At the same time, they try to adapt Jewish law to modern situations.

The reform group was first established in eighteenth century Europe. Most members moved to the United States. Reform Jews adapt their religion to modern needs. They see the old

Jewish laws and traditions as having no binding power over modern Jews. They gave up many of the practices and ceremonies of the Orthodox Jews.

Jewish people live all over the world. Historically, they have been unwilling to be counted. This makes it difficult to know the Jewish count exactly. It is estimated that there are between 12 and 14 million Jewish people worldwide. From a population perspective, Judaism is not even one of the top five world religions.

Reading from the Torah

HINDUISM

Another religion found in the Middle East is Hinduism. The Hindu religion began in the Indus Valley between 4000 and 2200 B.C. The Indus Valley is located in the northwestern part of India. It is recognized as the world's oldest organized religion. Hinduism is a henotheistic religion. That means that people who practice Hinduism believe in one supreme God. Hindus also recognize other gods as reflections of the one supreme God.

The most important god for Hindus is Brahma. Hindus believe that Brahma is the creator of everything. Vishnu, another Hindu god, preserves what Brahma created. The third god is Shiva, the destroyer.

Hindus have four simple goals. They are called the Four Aims of Hinduism. The first three are called the Pravritti. They tell a person how to live his/her life. The fourth goal is called the Nivritti. This goal is reached when a person dies. They are:

Pravritti:

1. Dharma: Live a good religious life. For Hindus, this is the most important rule.
2. Artha: Be successful. Acquire richness.
3. Kama: Feel good. Be happy and have sensual and mental enjoyment.

Nivritti:

4. Moksa: Freedom from suffering. When a person dies, he or she does not suffer anymore.

Hindus worship in temples and have more than one holy book. These teachings are found in them.

It is estimated that between 750 and 900 million people practice Hinduism throughout the world. That's about 13 percent of the world population. This makes the Hindu religion the third largest in the world. Hinduism is practiced in the Middle East in countries such as Pakistan and Kuwait.

Statue of the Hindu god, Vishnu, the preserver of creation.

DRUZE

Al-Hakim was the Egyptian ruler who founded the Druze religion in the early eleventh century. It started as a reform movement of Islam. Al-Hakim blended Islam's belief in one god with Greek thought and Hindu influences.

Since the middle of the eleventh century, this secretive religious community has been closed to outsiders. Those who are born Druze are not allowed to join another religion. Those who are not born into this religion are not allowed to become Druze. This practice likely explains why less than one percent of Middle Eastern people are Druze.

The Druze believe that God came to earth as al-Hakim. Al-Hakim disappeared in the year 1021. The majority of Muslims believe he died. The Druze believe he ascended into heaven. They believe he will return to earth when the time is right. They wait for him to make the world a wonderful place for true believers. Druze believe that al-Hakim is the one and only God. They also believe that the qualities of God can be found in all people.

The Druze religion was named for one of its earliest followers. His name was Muhammadu d-Darazi. Druze often live in the mountains. They do not drink alcohol, eat pork, or use tobacco. There is typically a strong sense of community among believers. They consider themselves to be members of the Muslim religion. Druze followers even believe they are the true messengers of the basic values of Islam.

The Druze recognize Judaism, Islam, and Christianity. In fact, the Druze prophets come from all three of these religions. They respect the meaning of the Koran, the Bible, and the writings of al-Hakim. Yet, the Druze believe the ceremonies and traditions of these faiths have caused Jews, Muslims, and Christians to turn away from "pure faith."

The Druze do not follow the Koran. They reject religious ceremonies and rituals. Instead of worshiping in mosques, they gather in khalwas. A khalwa is a simple temple that is decorated plainly. Druze have no set form of worship nor do they observe specific holy days. They do not set aside certain days for fasting. They do not take the pilgrimage to Mecca like other Muslims either. Most other Muslims do not think of the Druze as fellow Muslims.

Druze are led by five ministers. Each minister has a certain godly quality. These five ministers are represented in the symbol of the Druze star. Each point of the star is a different color and each color stands for a specific quality. The green point stands for the mind and the red for the soul. The yellow point stands for truth and the blue point for a person's will. The white stands for the material world.

The Druze religion has seven guidelines for living. They are:
1. Speak the truth.
2. Take care of one another.
3. Do not believe in any other religions.

Men worship inside Nabi Shueib, a Druze sacred site.

4. Stay away from the demon and people who do bad things.
5. Live in harmony with each other.
6. Accept all of al-Hakim's acts.
7. Act the way that al-Hakim would want you to.

Some people think that the Druze use a calf to represent the demon. It is believed that the Druze use the calf as a symbol of negative forces in the world.

The personal status of Druze women is much like that of Druze men. Druze women can hold important positions within their religion. In fact, the Druze believe women are more "spiritually prepared" than men.

The Druze believe that after death, people come back to earth in another body. The dead are given a new life. They believe that the quality of a person's life determines the quality of his/her future lives. A good person is believed to be rewarded with a good life again. Druze believe the opposite holds true for those who live a bad life.

There are an estimated 595,000 Druze followers living in the Middle East and North Africa. The majority of Druze in the Middle East live in Syria. However, some live in Israel, Jordan, and Lebanon.

Conclusion

The religions of the Middle East share some amazing similarities. They also differ enough from each other to cause conflict.

In the Israeli-Palestinian conflict, Muslim Arabs are angry with the Israeli Jews for making the former nation of Palestine theirs. The city of Jerusalem, especially, has been the source of much friction between the Jews and the Muslims. People of both religions consider it holy land. In 1950, Israel claimed Jerusalem as its capital. Palestinians and other Arabs were angered about losing land to the Jews. Other Arab nations still support Palestinians in opposing Israel. What unites the Arabs is their Islamic religion. The Muslims resent non-Muslims living on Arab land.

The Middle East has also witnessed conflict between Muslims and Christians. In 1975, war broke out in Lebanon between the Christian majority and the Muslims. Muslims felt that the Christians were not sharing power or economic opportunities with them.

The country of Iran witnessed the overthrow of its government in 1979. Radical Islamic fundamentalists, led by the Ayatollah Khomeini, took over the government. This group did not like the cozy relationship the former government had with the West. The fundamentalists resented Western influence on Arab people. Khomeini led an Islamic fundamentalist government in Iran from 1979 until his death in 1989.

Just months before Khomeini's death, he called for the killing of an author named Salman Rushdie. Khomeini was angered by the way Rushdie portrayed the Islamic religion and its leader, the Prophet Muhammad, in his book of fiction, *The Satanic Verses*. Rushdie was forced into hiding for years until the death threat was officially canceled.

An Islamic fundamentalist group called the Taliban took control of Afghanistan in 1996. Its leader, Mullah Omar, demanded that all pre-Islamic statues and shrines in Afghanistan be destroyed. Centuries-old Buddhist statues were blown up. Omar felt he was right in implementing Islamic order.

The fighting between the Jews and the Muslims continues. The Israeli government continues to bulldoze the homes of Palestinians who oppose it. The Palestinians continue to fight back with terroristic acts, such as suicide bombings.

Tolerance and the need to understand all religions is as important now as ever before. Without understanding, unnecessary death and destruction will continue.

Druze Men

TIMELINE

4000 – 2000 B.C.	The Hindu religion begins in the Indus Valley in India. (The exact year is unknown.)
2000 – 1700	Abraham, the spiritual founder of Judaism, Christianity, and Islam is born in Mesopotamia. Abraham is chosen by God to tell all people about monotheism. (The exact year is unknown.)
4 B.C. – 0	Jesus, believed by Christians to be the son of God, is born in Bethlehem. (The exact year is unknown.)
30s	Jesus is crucified and is said to be resurrected from the dead. (The exact year is unknown.)
313	The Roman Empire recognizes Christianity as a real religion.
325	Christianity becomes the official religion of the Roman Empire.
570	The Muslim Prophet Muhammad is born in Mecca, Saudi Arabia.

622	The Prophet Muhammad and his followers settle in Medina, Saudi Arabia. The Muslim lunar calendar is set by this date.
1000s	Egyptian ruler, al-Hakim, founds the Druze religion. He disappears in the year 1021. Followers believe he was taken to heaven.
1948	Middle East Jews claim Israel as an independent nation. The fighting between Middle East Muslims and Jews begins.
1950	Israel claims Jerusalem as its capital.
1975	War breaks out in Lebanon between the Christian majority and the growing Muslim population.
1979 – 1989	Islamic fundamentalism takes hold in Iran after Khomeini and his followers overthrow the government.
1989	The Ayatollah Khomeini calls for the death of Salman Rushdie.
2001	Mullah Omar, leader of the Taliban regime, demands that all pre-Islamic statues and shrines in Afghanistan be destroyed.
2003	Fighting between Israelis and Arabs continues.

Statue of Brahma, the Hindu god of creation

FAST FACTS

- Hinduism is recognized as the world's oldest organized religion and the third most practiced religion.
- Three of the major world religions, Judaism, Christianity, and Islam, all view Abraham as their religion's first prophet.
- Judaism, Christianity, and Islam are all monotheistic religions. This means that each believes that only one god exists.
- There are more Muslims living in the Middle East than all the other religions combined.
- The Druze consider themselves the "true Muslims." Other Muslims don't accept the Druze as fellow Muslims.
- The Gregorian calendar is used in most Western nations today. It was set by the approximate year of Jesus' birth and is based on the cycles of the sun.
- The Islamic calendar was set by the Prophet Muhammad's move from Mecca to Medina. It is based on the cycles of the moon.
- The Hebrew calendar is made up of two different cycles. The religious cycle begins in spring, while the civil cycle begins in fall.
- Each year, Muslims are expected to give at least 2.2 percent of their wealth to the poor.
- Mecca was a holy city even before the birth of Muhammad.
- The Christian Bible contains the first five books of the Jewish holy book, which is called the Torah.

WEB SITES
WWW.ABDOPUB.COM

Would you like to learn more about Religions of the Middle East? Please visit www.abdopub.com to find up-to-date Web site links about Religions of the Middle East and the World in Conflict. These links are routinely monitored and updated to provide the most current information available.

A symbol of the Islamic religion

GLOSSARY

adultery: Having sexual relations with someone other than a spouse while being married.

ascended: To go or move upward; to rise.

Baptist: A Christian denomination.

caliph: A male Islamic leader who is regarded as a successor to Muhammad.

category: A specifically defined division of a larger group; a subset.

Catholic: A member of a Catholic church, including a Roman Catholic.

communion: Spiritual fellowship.

conceive: To become pregnant.

concentration camp: A place where citizens become prisoners of war under harsh conditions.

covet: To strongly desire for that which is another's.

demon: An evil, supernatural being; a devil.

dictatorship: Absolute control or power by an individual.

divine: Heavenly.

Egypt: A country in the Middle East that is part of northeast Africa.

Emperor Constantine: The emperor who converted the Roman Empire to Christianity. Before his conversion, the Romans worshiped many gods.

Evangelical: Relating to Christians who believe the Bible is never wrong.

everlasting: Lasting forever.

extremist: One who advocates or resorts to measures beyond the norm, especially in politics or religion.

Germany: A country in north-central Europe.

governor: A person who governs.

Gregorian calendar: The solar calendar in use throughout most of the world, sponsored by Pope Gregory XIII in 1582. This calendar is set by the approximate year of Jesus' birth.

heaven: Some religions believe this is a place in or beyond the sky where God dwells.

hell: Some religions believe this is the place where evil dwells.

Holy Spirit: Christians believe that this is one of the forms through which God reveals himself to humans.

intolerance: Unwillingness to recognize and respect differences in opinions or beliefs.

Iraq: A country in the Middle East.

Israeli-Palestinian Conflict: Conflict over land between Israelis and Palestinians.

Jerusalem: Both Israelis and Palestinians consider Jerusalem their capital.

Kuwait: A country in the Middle East.

Lebanon: A country in the Middle East.

Lutheran: A Christian denomination.

millionaire: A person whose wealth amounts to at least a million dollars, pounds, or the equivalent in another currency.

Pakistan: A country in the Middle East.

pilgrimage: The journey to a holy place.

plague: A sudden destructive force or outbreak that causes harm.

Pontius Pilate: Roman Governor who ordered the crucifixion of Jesus.

Presbyterian: A Christian denomination.

prosperity: Material wealth.

Ramadan: The ninth month of the year in the Islamic calendar.

rededicate: To dedicate is to set something apart for religious purposes. It is a way to show honor to God. To rededicate, is to dedicate something again after the first dedication.

resurrection: The act of rising from the dead or returning to life.

Rome: Capital of the Roman Empire in Europe.

Sabbath: A weekly day of rest required by God of Abraham's followers.

sacred: Holy.

Scripture: A sacred writing or book.

sect: A group of people forming a distinct unit within a larger group.

sensual: Relating to any of the five senses. Also suggests sexuality.

shalt: Biblical way of saying "should."

successor: One that succeeds, or comes after, another.

Syria: A country in the Middle East.

terrorist: One who engages in acts or an act of terrorism.

tradition: The passing down of cultural elements from generation to generation.

United Nations (UN): An international organization composed of most of the countries of the world. It was founded in 1945 to promote peace, security, and economic development.

INDEX